THE
SPIRIT-FILLED
POCKET BIBLE
ON
FINANCES

THE
SPIRIT-FILLED
POCKET BIBLE
ON
FINANCES

HARRISON HOUSE, INC.
Tulsa, Oklahoma

2nd Printing
Over 15,000 in Print

The Spirit-Filled Pocket Bible on Finances
ISBN 0-89274-835-4
Copyright © 1995 by Harrison House, Inc.
P. O. Box 35035
Tulsa, Oklahoma 74153

Published by Harrison House, Inc.
P. O. Box 35035
Tulsa, Oklahoma 74153

The
Spirit-Filled
Pocket Bible
on Finances

Presented to

_____

By

_____

Date

_____

Introduction

This is a time, as never before, to be hooked into God's economic system. While God's financial principles for a stable economy do not fluctuate, the world's economic system changes from day to day.

With God's principles, it is possible to reap a hundredfold return on your giving into His Kingdom, even in the midst of a natural famine, just as Isaac experienced. (Genesis 26:12.) It is possible to remain blessed in the midst of a world economy that is in great turmoil.

The financial principles presented in the Old and New Testament accounts contained in this book *The Spirit-Filled Pocket Bible on Finances* will strengthen your knowledge of God's principles for being a part of a flourishing economy. These principles will guide you into the *increase* God has planned for your life. They will serve as a guide in all of your financial affairs, enabling you to represent Jesus with highest integrity.

The key to success in every area of your life — including finances, which is our focus in this book — is found in

Joshua 1:8 (*Moffatt's Trans.*):

"This lawbook you shall never cease to have on your lips; you must pore over it day and night, that you may be mindful to carry out all that is written in it, *for so shall you make your way prosperous, so shall you succeed.*"

Opportunity awaits you to step into a higher level of financial responsibility, integrity and abundance as you meditate continually on the Scriptures in this book.

Prayer

Heavenly Father, thank You for Your guidance in directing me to new financial goals for increase, investing and giving of tithes, offerings and alms, in Jesus' name.

Thank You that a spirit of wisdom and understanding, counsel and might and knowledge and reverential fear of You, Lord, guide me in all of my financial affairs. (Isaiah 11:2.)

Thank You, Lord, that Your Spirit causes me to be bold as a lion (Proverbs 28:1) in obeying Your directives so that I can receive the release of wealth that You desire to entrust to me.

Father, thank You for Your Word, which renews my mind from a poverty mentality to one of unlimited abundance. I receive Your will for my life in every area, Lord, which is life more abundantly (John 10:10) and unlimited prosperity in my spirit, soul (which includes the mind, will and emotions) and body. (3 John 2.)

Because I am seeking first Your Kingdom and Your righteousness, Lord, all of the things which I need are added unto me. (Matthew 6:33.)

Thank You, Lord, that not only are my needs met, but I am a recipient of the wealth of the wicked (Proverbs 13:22) in this very hour, so I can be a major contributor to the evangelization of the world — bringing Your message of saving grace, healing, deliverance, restoration, preservation and soundness to others.

Thank You for being faithful to all of the promises of Your Word, Father, in Jesus' name. Amen.

FINANCIAL SCRIPTURES

Financial Scriptures

While the earth remaineth, *seedtime and harvest*, and cold and heat, and summer and winter, and day and night shall not cease.

Genesis 8:22

And God blessed Noah and his sons, and said unto them, Be fruitful, and multiply, and replenish the earth.

Genesis 9:1

And I will make of thee a great nation, and I will bless thee, and make thy name great; and thou shalt be a blessing:

And I will bless them that bless thee, and curse him that curseth thee: and in thee shall all families of the earth be blessed.

Genesis 12:2,3

Then Melchizedek king of Salem brought out bread and wine. He was priest of God Most High, and he blessed Abram, saying, "Blessed be Abram by God Most High, Creator of heaven and earth.

13

"And blessed be God Most High, who delivered your enemies into your hand." Then Abram gave him a tenth of everything.

The king of Sodom said to Abram, "Give me the people and keep the goods for yourself."

But Abram said to the king of Sodom, "I have raised my hand to the Lord, God Most High, Creator of heaven and earth, and have taken an oath that I will accept nothing belonging to you, not even a thread or the thong of a sandal, so that you will never be able to say, 'I made Abram rich.' I will accept nothing but what my men have eaten and the share that belongs to the men who went with me — to Aner, Eshcol and Mamre. Let them have their share."

Genesis 14:18-24 NIV

When Abram was ninety-nine years old, the Lord appeared to him and said, "I am God Almighty; walk before me and be blameless. I will confirm my covenant between me and you and will greatly increase your numbers."

Abram fell facedown, and God said to him, "As for me, this is my covenant with you: You will be the father of many nations. No longer will you be called Abram; your name will be Abraham, for I have made you a father of many nations. I will make you very fruitful; I will make nations of you, and kings will come from you. I will establish my covenant as an everlasting covenant between me and you and your descendants after you for the generations to come, to be your God and the God of your descendants after you.

Genesis 17:1-7 NIV

And God said unto Abraham, As for Sarai thy wife, thou shalt not call her name Sarai, but Sarah shall her name be.

And I will bless her, and give thee a son also of her: yea, I will bless her, and she shall be a mother of nations; kings of people shall be of her.

Genesis 17:15,16

And the Lord said, Shall I hide from Abraham that thing which I do;

Seeing that Abraham shall surely become a great and mighty nation, and all the nations of the earth shall be blessed in him?

For I know him, that he will command his children and his household after him, and they shall keep the way of the Lord, to do justice and judgment; that the Lord may bring upon Abraham that which he hath spoken of him.

Genesis 18:17-19

Then the angel of the Lord called to Abraham a second time from heaven,

And said, "By Myself I have sworn," declares the Lord, "because you have done this thing, and have not withheld your son, your only son,

"Indeed I will greatly bless you, and I will greatly multiply your seed as the stars of the heavens, and as the sand which is on the seashore; and your seed shall possess the gate of their enemies.

"And in your seed all the nations of the earth shall be blessed, because you have obeyed My voice."

Genesis 22:15-18 NASB

And Abraham was old, and well stricken in age: and the Lord had blessed Abraham in all things.

Genesis 24:1

And there was a famine in the land, beside the first famine that was in the days of Abraham. And Isaac went unto Abimelech king of the Philistines unto Gerar.

And the Lord appeared unto him, and said, Go not down into Egypt; dwell in the land which I shall tell thee of:

Sojourn in this land, and I will be with thee, and will bless thee; for unto thee, and unto thy seed, I will give all these countries, and I will perform the oath which I sware unto Abraham thy father;

And I will make thy seed to multiply as the stars of heaven, and will give unto thy seed all these countries; and in thy seed shall all the nations of the earth be blessed;

Because that Abraham obeyed my voice, and kept my charge, my commandments, my statutes, and my laws.

Genesis 26:1-5

Isaac sowed a crop in that country and

reaped in the same year a hundredfold.
The Eternal blessed him; he grew rich and
increased till he became very rich, with
property in flocks and herds and a large
household.

Genesis 26:12-14
Moffatt's Trans.

I am the God of your father Abraham: fear
not, I am with you and I will bless you and
multiply your descendants, for the sake of
my servant Abraham.

Genesis 26:24
Moffatt's Trans.

And God Almighty bless thee, and make
thee fruitful, and multiply thee, that thou
mayest be a multitude of people.

Genesis 28:3

And the man [Jacob] increased exceedingly, and had much cattle, and maidservants,
and menservants, and camels, and asses.

Genesis 30:43

Joseph is a fruitful vine, a fruitful vine
near a spring, whose branches climb over a
wall.

With bitterness archers attacked him; they shot at him with hostility.

But his bow remained steady, his strong arms stayed limber, because of the hand of the Mighty One of Jacob, because of the Shepherd, the Rock of Israel,

Because of your father's God, who helps you, because of the Almighty, who blesses you with blessings of the heavens above, blessings of the deep that lies below, blessings of the breast and womb.

Your father's blessings are greater than the blessings of the ancient mountains, than the bounty of the age-old hills. Let all these rest on the head of Joseph, on the brow of the prince among his brothers.

Genesis 49:22-26 NIV

And the Lord said, I have surely seen the affliction of my people which are in Egypt, and have heard their cry by reason of their taskmasters; for I know their sorrows;

And I am come down to deliver them out of the hand of the Egyptians, and to bring them up out of that land unto a good land and a large, unto a land flowing with milk and honey.

Exodus 3:7,8a

And ye shall serve the Lord your God, and he shall bless thy bread, and thy water.

Exodus 23:25a

So Bezalel, Oholiab and every skilled person to whom the Lord has given skill and ability to know how to carry out all the work of constructing the sanctuary are to do the work just as the Lord has commanded.

Then Moses summoned Bezalel and Oholiab and every skilled person to whom the Lord had given ability and who was willing to come and do the work. They received from Moses all the offerings the Israelites had brought to carry out the work of constructing the sanctuary. And the people continued to bring freewill offerings morning after morning. So all the skilled craftsmen who were doing all the work on the sanctuary left their work and said to Moses, "The people are bringing more than enough for doing the work the Lord commanded to be done."

Then Moses gave an order and they

sent this word throughout the camp: "No man or woman is to make anything else as an offering for the sanctuary." And so the people were restrained from bringing more, because what they already had was more than enough to do all the work.

Exodus 36:1-7 NIV

If you walk in My statutes and keep My commandments so as to carry them out,

Then I shall give you rains in their season, so that the land will yield its produce and the trees of the field will bear their fruit.

Indeed, your threshing will last for you until grape gathering, and grape gathering will last until sowing time. You will thus eat your food to the full and live securely in your land.

I shall also grant peace in the land, so that you may lie down with no one making you tremble. I shall also eliminate harmful beasts from the land, and no sword will pass through your land.

But you will chase your enemies, and they will fall before you by the sword;

Five of you will chase a hundred, and

a hundred of you will chase ten thousand, and your enemies will fall before you by the sword.

So I will turn toward you and make you fruitful and multiply you, and I will confirm My covenant with you.

And you will eat the old supply and clear out the old because of the new.

Moreover, I will make My dwelling among you, and My soul will not reject you.

I will also walk among you and be your God, and you shall be My people.

I am the Lord your God, who brought you out of the land of Egypt so that you should not be their slaves, and I broke the bars of your yoke and made you walk erect.

Leviticus 26:3-13 NASB

And all the tithe of the land, whether of the seed of the land or of the fruit of the tree, is the Lord's. It is holy to the Lord.

If a man wants at all to redeem any of his tithes, he shall add one-fifth to it.

And concerning the tithe of the herd

or the flock, of whatever passes under the rod, the tenth one shall be holy to the Lord.

He shall not inquire whether it is good or bad, nor shall he exchange it; and if he exchanges it at all, then both it and the one exchanged for it shall be holy; it shall not be redeemed.

These are the commandments which the Lord commanded Moses for the children of Israel on Mount Sinai.

Leviticus 27:30-34 NKJV

May the Lord bless and protect you; may the Lord's face radiate with joy because of you; may he be gracious to you, show you his favor, and give you his peace. This is how Aaron and his sons shall call down my blessings upon the people of Israel; and I myself will personally bless them.

Numbers 6:24-27 TLB

If the Lord delight in us, then he will bring us into this land, and give it us; a land which floweth with milk and honey.

Numbers 14:8

23

And the Lord spake unto Moses, saying,

Thus speak unto the Levites, and say unto them, When ye take of the children of Israel the tithes which I have given you from them for your inheritance, then ye shall offer up an heave offering of it for the Lord, even a tenth part of the tithe.

And this your heave offering shall be reckoned unto you, as though it were the corn of the threshingfloor, and as the fulness of the winepress.

Thus ye also shall offer an heave offering unto the Lord of all your tithes, which ye receive of the children of Israel; and ye shall give thereof the Lord's heave offering to Aaron the priest.

Out of all your gifts ye shall offer every heave offering of the Lord, of all the best thereof, even the hallowed part thereof out of it.

Therefore thou shalt say unto them, When ye have heaved the best thereof from it, then it shall be counted unto the Levites as the increase of the threshingfloor, and as the increase of the winepress.

And ye shall eat it in every place, ye and your households: for it is your reward for your service in the tabernacle of the congregation.

And ye shall bear no sin by reason of it, when ye have heaved from it the best of it: neither shall ye pollute the holy things of the children of Israel, lest ye die.

Numbers 18:25-32

God is not a man, that he should lie; neither the son of man, that he should repent: hath he said, and shall he not do it? or hath he spoken, and shall he not make it good?

Behold, I have received commandment to bless: and he hath blessed; and I cannot reverse it.

Numbers 23:19,20

There it lies; march in and take possession of the land that the Eternal swore he would give to your fathers, Abraham, Isaac, and Jacob, and to their descendants.

Then it was that I told you, "I cannot bear the burden of you single-handed. The Eternal your God has multiplied you, till now your numbers are like the stars in the sky. (May the Eternal the God of your fathers multiply you still a thousand-fold, and prosper you as he promised you!)"

Deuteronomy 1:8-11
Moffatt's Trans.

For the Lord your God has blessed you in all the work of your hand. He knows your walking through this great wilderness. These forty years the Lord your God has been with you; you have lacked nothing.

Deuteronomy 2:7 AMP

Know therefore that the Lord thy God, he is God, the faithful God, which keepeth covenant and mercy with them that love him and keep his commandments to a thousand generations.

Deuteronomy 7:9

Wherefore it shall come to pass, if ye hearken to these judgments, and keep, and do them, that the Lord thy God shall keep unto thee the covenant and the mercy which he sware unto thy fathers:

And he will love thee, and bless thee, and multiply thee: he will also bless the fruit of thy womb, and the fruit of thy land, thy corn, and thy wine, and thine oil, the increase of thy kine, and the flocks of thy sheep, in the land which he sware unto thy fathers to give thee.

Thou shalt be blessed above all people: there shall not be male or female barren among you, or among your cattle.

Deuteronomy 7:12-14

Observe the commands of the Lord your God, walking in his ways and revering him. For the Lord your God is bringing you into a good land — a land with streams and pools of water, with springs flowing in the valleys and hills; a land with wheat and barley, vines and fig trees, pomegranates, olive oil and honey; a land where bread will not be scarce and you will lack nothing; a land where the rocks are iron and you can dig copper out of the hills.

When you have eaten and are satisfied, praise the Lord your God for the good land he has given you. Be careful that you do not forget the Lord your God, failing to observe his commands, his laws and his decrees that I am giving you this day. Otherwise, when you eat and are satisfied, when you build fine houses and settle down, and when your herds and flocks grow large and your silver and gold increase and all you have is multiplied, then your heart will become proud and you will forget the Lord your God, who brought you out of Egypt, out the land of slavery. He led you through the vast and dreadful desert, that thirsty and waterless land, with its venomous snakes and scorpions. He brought you water out of hard rock. He gave you manna to eat in the desert, something your fathers had never known, to humble and to test you so that in the end it might go well with you. You may say to yourself, "My power and the strength of my hands have produced this wealth for me." But remember the Lord your God, for it is he who gives you the ability to produce wealth, and so confirms

his covenant, which he swore to your forefathers, as it is today.

Deuteronomy 8:6-18 NIV

Therefore shall ye keep all the commandments which I command you this day, that
ye may be strong, and go in and possess
the land, whither ye go to possess it;

And that ye may prolong your days in
the land, which the Lord sware unto your
fathers to give unto them and to their
seed, a land that floweth with milk and
honey.

Deuteronomy 11:8,9

And there ye shall eat before the Lord
your God, and ye shall rejoice in all that ye
put your hand unto, ye and your households, wherein the Lord thy God hath
blessed thee.

Deuteronomy 12:7

You shall surely tithe all the produce from
what you sow, which comes out of the
field every year.

Deuteronomy 14:22 NASB

At the end of every third year you shall bring out all the tithe of your produce in that year, and shall deposit it in your town.

And the Levite, because he has no portion or inheritance among you, and the alien, the orphan and the widow who are in your town, shall come and eat and be satisfied, in order that the Lord your God may bless you in all the work of your hand which you do.

Deuteronomy 14:28,29 NASB

At the end of every seven years thou shalt make a release.

And this is the manner of the release: Every creditor that lendeth ought unto his neighbour shall release it; he shall not exact it of his neighbour, or of his brother; because it is called the Lord's release.

Of a foreigner thou mayest exact it again: but that which is thine with thy brother thine hand shall release;

Save when there shall be no poor among you; for the Lord shall greatly bless thee in the land which the Lord thy God giveth thee for an inheritance to possess it:

Only if thou carefully hearken unto

the voice of the Lord thy God, to observe to do all these commandments which I command thee this day.

For the Lord thy God blesseth thee, as he promised thee: and thou shalt lend unto many nations, but thou shalt not borrow; and thou shalt reign over many nations, but they shall not reign over thee.

If there be among you a poor man of one of thy brethren within any of thy gates in thy land which the Lord thy God giveth thee, thou shalt not harden thine heart, nor shut thine hand from thy poor brother:

But thou shalt open thine hand wide unto him, and shalt surely lend him sufficient for his need, in that which he wanteth.

Beware that there be not a thought in thy wicked heart, saying, The seventh year, the year of release, is at hand; and thine eye be evil against thy poor brother, and thou givest him nought; and he cry unto the Lord against thee, and it be sin unto thee.

Thou shalt surely give him, and thine heart shall not be grieved when thou givest unto him: because that for this thing the Lord thy God shall bless thee in all thy works, and in all that thou puttest thine hand unto.

For the poor shall never cease out of the land: therefore I command thee, saying, Thou shalt open thine hand wide unto thy brother, to thy poor, and to thy needy, in thy land.

Deuteronomy 15:1-11

Every man shall give as he is able, according to the blessing of the Lord thy God which he hath given thee.

Deuteronomy 16:17

When you make a vow to the Lord your God, you shall not delay to pay it, for it would be sin in you, and the Lord your God will surely require it of you.

However, if you refrain from vowing, it would not be sin in you.

You shall be careful to perform what goes out from your lips, just as you have voluntarily vowed to the Lord your God, what you have promised.

Deuteronomy 23:21-23 NASB

When you have finished setting aside a tenth of all your produce in the third year, the year of the tithe, you shall give it to the Levite, the alien, the fatherless and the widow, so that they may eat in your towns and be satisfied.

Then say to the Lord your God: "I have removed from my house the sacred portion and have given it to the Levite, the alien, the fatherless and the widow, according to all you commanded. I have not turned aside from your commands nor have I forgotten any of them.

I have not eaten any of the sacred portion while I was in mourning, nor have I removed any of it while I was unclean, nor have I offered any of it to the dead. I have obeyed the Lord my God; I have done everything you commanded me.

Look down from heaven, your holy dwelling place, and bless your people Israel and the land you have given us as you promised on oath to our forefathers, a land flowing with milk and honey."

The Lord your God commands you this day to follow these decrees and laws; carefully observe them with all your heart and with all your soul.

You have declared this day that the Lord is your God and that you will walk in his ways, that you will keep his decrees, commands and laws, and that you will obey him.

And the Lord has declared this day that you are his people, his treasured possession as he promised, and that you are to keep all his commands.

He has declared that he will set you in praise, fame and honor high above all the nations he has made and that you will be a people holy to the Lord your God, as he promised.

Deuteronomy 26:12-19 NIV

If you fully obey the Lord your God and carefully follow all his commands I give you today, the Lord your God will set you high above all the nations on earth. All these blessings will come upon you and accompany you if you obey the Lord your God:

You will be blessed in the city and blessed in the country.

The fruit of your womb will be

blessed, and the crops of your land and the young of your livestock — the calves of your herds and the lambs of your flocks.

Your basket and your kneading trough will be blessed.

You will be blessed when you come in and blessed when you go out.

The Lord will grant that the enemies who rise up against you will be defeated before you. They will come at you from one direction but flee from you in seven.

The Lord will send a blessing on your barns and on everything you put your hand to. The Lord your God will bless you in the land he is giving you.

The Lord will establish you as his holy people, as he promised you on oath, if you keep the commands of the Lord your God and walk in his ways. Then all the peoples on earth will see that you are called by the name of the Lord, and they will fear you. The Lord will grant you abundant prosperity — in the fruit of your womb, the young of your livestock and the crops of your ground — in the land he swore to your forefathers to give you.

The Lord will open the heavens, the storehouse of his bounty, to send rain on your land in season and to bless all the work of your hands. You will lend to many nations but will borrow from none. The Lord will make you the head, not the tail. If you pay attention to the commands of the Lord your God that I give you this day and carefully follow them, you will always be at the top, never at the bottom. Do not turn aside from any of the commands I give you today, to the right hand or to the left, following other gods and serving them.

Deuteronomy 28:1-14 NIV

Keep therefore the words of this covenant, and do them, that ye may prosper in all that ye do.

Deuteronomy 29:9

And the Lord thy God will make thee plenteous in every work of thine hand, in the fruit of thy body, and in the fruit of thy cattle, and in the fruit of thy land, for good: for the Lord will again rejoice over thee for good, as he rejoiced over thy fathers:

If thou shalt hearken unto the voice of the Lord thy God, to keep his commandments and his statutes which are written in this book of the law, and if thou turn unto the Lord thy God with all thine heart, and with all thy soul.

Deuteronomy 30:9,10

See, I have set before thee this day life and good, and death and evil;

In that I command thee this day to love the Lord thy God, to walk in his ways, and to keep his commandments and his statutes, and his judgments, that thou mayest live and multiply: and the Lord thy God shall bless thee in the land whither thou goest to possess it.

Deuteronomy 30:15,16

I call heaven and earth to record this day against you, that I have set before you life and death, blessing and cursing: therefore choose life, that both thou and thy seed may live:

That thou mayest love the Lord thy God, and that thou mayest obey his voice, and that thou mayest cleave unto him: for he is thy life, and the length of thy days: that thou mayest dwell in the land which the Lord sware unto thy fathers, to Abraham, to Isaac, and to Jacob, to give them.

Deuteronomy 30:19,20

Every place that the sole of your foot shall tread upon, that have I given unto you, as I said unto Moses.

Joshua 1:3

Only be thou strong and very courageous, that thou mayest observe to do according to all the law, which Moses my servant commanded thee: turn not from it to the right hand or to the left, that thou mayest prosper whithersoever thou goest.

This book of the law shall not depart out of thy mouth; but thou shalt meditate therein day and night, that thou mayest observe to do according to all that is written therein: for then thou shalt make thy way prosperous, and then thou shalt have good success.

Joshua 1:7,8

And now, O Lord God, thou art that God, and thy words be true, and thou hast promised this goodness unto thy servant:

Therefore now let it please thee to bless the house of thy servant, that it may continue for ever before thee: for thou, O Lord God, hast spoken it: and with thy blessing let the house of thy servant be blessed for ever.

2 Samuel 7:28,29

The wife of a man from the company of the prophets cried out to Elisha, "Your servant my husband is dead, and you know that he revered the Lord. But now his creditor is coming to take my two boys as his slaves."

Elisha replied to her, "How can I help you? Tell me, *what do you have in your house?*"

"Your servant has nothing there at all," she said, "except a little oil."

Elisha said, "Go around and ask all your neighbors for empty jars. Don't ask for just a few. Then go inside and shut the door behind you and your sons. Pour oil into all the jars, and as each is filled, put it to one side."

She left him and afterward shut the door behind her and her sons. They brought the jars to her and she kept pouring. When all the jars were full, she said to her son, "Bring me another one."

But he replied, "There is not a jar left." Then the oil stopped flowing.

She went and told the man of God, and he said, "Go, sell the oil and pay your debts. You and your sons can live on what is left."

2 Kings 4:1-7 NIV

And now, Lord, thou art God, and hast promised this goodness unto thy servant:

Now therefore let it please thee to bless the house of thy servant, that it may be before thee for ever: for thou blessest, O Lord, and it shall be blessed for ever.

1 Chronicles 17:26,27

Only the Lord give thee wisdom and understanding, and give thee charge concerning Israel, that thou mayest keep the law of the Lord thy God.

Then shalt thou prosper, if thou takest heed to fulfil the statutes and judgments which the Lord charged Moses with concerning Israel: be strong, and of good courage; dread not, nor be dismayed.

1 Chronicles 22:12,13

Both riches and honour come of thee, and thou reignest over all; and in thine hand is power and might; and in thine hand it is to make great, and to give strength unto all.

1 Chronicles 29:12

And he [David] died in a good old age, full of days, riches, and honour.

1 Chronicles 29:28a

Now Jehoshaphat had riches and honour in abundance.

2 Chronicles 18:1a

Believe in the Lord your God, so shall ye be established; believe his prophets, so shall ye prosper.

2 Chronicles 20:20b

41

And he [Uzziah] did that which was right in the sight of the Lord, according to all that his father Amaziah did.

And he sought God in the days of Zechariah, who had understanding in the visions of God: and as long as he sought the Lord, God made him to prosper.

2 Chronicles 26:4,5

Moreover, he commanded the people that dwelt in Jerusalem to give the portion of the priests and the Levites, that they might be encouraged in the law of the Lord.

And as soon as the commandment came abroad, the children of Israel brought in abundance the firstfruits of corn, wine, and oil, and honey, and of all the increase of the field; and the tithe of all things brought they in abundantly.

And concerning the children of Israel and Judah, that dwelt in the cities of Judah, they also brought in the tithe of oxen and sheep, and the tithe of holy things which were consecrated unto the Lord their God, and laid them by heaps.

In the third month they began to lay the foundation of the heaps, and finished them in the seventh month.

And when Hezekiah and the princes came and saw the heaps, they blessed the Lord, and his people Israel.

Then Hezekiah questioned with the priests and the Levites concerning the heaps.

And Azariah the chief priest of the house of Zadok answered him, and said, Since the people began to bring the offerings into the house of the Lord, we have had enough to eat, and have left plenty: for the Lord hath blessed his people; and that which is left is this great store.

Then Hezekiah commanded to prepare chambers in the house of the Lord; and they prepared them,

And brought in the offerings and the tithes and the dedicated things faithfully.

2 Chronicles 31:4-12a

And thus did Hezekiah throughout all Judah, and wrought that which was good and right and truth before the Lord his God.

And in every work that he began in the service of the house of God, and in the

law, and in the commandments, to seek
his God, he did it with all his heart, and
prospered.

2 Chronicles 31:20,21

I answered them, The God of heaven will
prosper us: therefore we His servants will
arise and build.

Nehemiah 2:20a AMP

Indeed, forty years Thou didst provide for
them in the wilderness and they were not
in want, their clothes did not wear out,
nor did their feet swell.

Thou didst also give them kingdoms
and peoples, and Thou didst allot them to
them as a boundary. And they took possession of the land of Sihon the king of
Heshbon, and the land of Og the king of
Bashan.

And Thou didst make their sons
numerous as the stars of heaven, and
Thou didst bring them into the land
which Thou hadst told their fathers to
enter and possess.

So their sons entered and possessed

the land. And Thou didst subdue before them the inhabitants of the land, the Canaanites, and Thou didst give them into their hand, with their kings, and the peoples of the land, to do with them as they desired.

And they captured fortified cities and a fertile land. They took possession of houses full of every good thing, hewn cisterns, vineyards, olive groves, fruit trees in abundance. So they ate, were filled, and grew fat, and reveled in Thy great goodness.

Nehemiah 9:21-25 NASB

Your beginnings will seem humble, so prosperous will your future be.

Job 8:7 NIV

If thou return to the Almighty, thou shalt be built up, thou shalt put away iniquity far from thy tabernacles.

Then shalt thou lay up gold as dust, and the gold of Ophir as the stones of the brooks.

Yea, the Almighty shall be thy defence, and thou shalt have plenty of silver.

For then shalt thou have thy delight in the Almighty, and shalt lift up thy face unto God.

Thou shalt make thy prayer unto him, and he shall hear thee, and thou shalt pay thy vows.

Thou shalt also decree a thing, and it shall be established unto thee: and the light shall shine upon thy ways.

Job 22:23-28

If they obey and serve him, they shall spend their days in prosperity, and their years in pleasures.

Job 36:11

The Lord blessed the latter part of Job's life more than the first. He had fourteen thousand sheep, six thousand camels, a thousand yoke of oxen and a thousand donkeys. And he also had seven sons and three daughters...

After this, Job lived a hundred and forty years; he saw his children and their children to the fourth generation. And so he died, old and full of years.

Job 42:12,13,16,17 NIV

Blessed is the man that walketh not in the counsel of the ungodly, nor standeth in the way of sinners, nor sitteth in the seat of the scornful.

But his delight is in the law of the Lord; and in his law doth he meditate day and night.

And he shall be like a tree planted by the rivers of water, that bringeth forth his fruit in his season; his leaf also shall not wither; and whatsoever he doeth shall prosper.

Psalm 1:1-3

Happy the man who never goes by the advice of the ungodly, who never takes the sinners' road, nor joins the company of scoffers,

But finds his joy in the Eternal's law, poring over it day and night.

He is like a tree planted by a stream, that bears fruit in due season, with leaves that never fade; whatever he does, he prospers.

Psalm 1:1-3
Moffatt's Trans.

May your blessing be on your people.
Psalm 3:8b NIV

For you, Lord, will bless the [uncompro-
misingly] righteous [him who is upright
and in right standing with You]; as with a
shield You will surround him with good-
will (pleasure and favor).
Psalm 5:12 AMP

For thou wilt bless the just, O thou
Eternal, shielding them safe, crowning
them with thy favour.
Psalm 5:12
Moffatt's Trans.

The law of the Lord is perfect, restoring
the [whole] person; the testimony of the
Lord is sure, making wise the simple.

The precepts of the Lord are right, re-
joicing the heart; the commandment of
the Lord is pure and bright, enlightening
the eyes.

The [reverent] fear of the Lord is
clean, enduring forever; the ordinances of
the Lord are true and righteous altogether.

More to be desired are they than gold, even than much fine gold; they are sweeter also than honey and the drippings from the honeycomb.

Moreover, by them is Your servant warned (reminded, illuminated, and instructed); and in keeping them there is great reward.

Psalm 19:7-11 AMP

The Lord is my Shepherd [to feed, guide, and shield me], I shall not lack.

He makes me lie down in [fresh, tender] green pastures; He leads me beside the still and restful waters.

He refreshes and restores my life (my self); He leads me in the paths of righteousness [uprightness and right standing with Him — not for my earning it, but] for His name's sake.

Yes, though I walk through the [deep, sunless] valley of the shadow of death, I will fear or dread no evil, for You are with me: Your rod [to protect] and Your staff [to guide], they comfort me.

You prepare a table before me in the presence of my enemies. You anoint my head with oil; my [brimming] cup runs over.

Surely or only goodness, mercy, and unfailing love shall follow me all the days of my life, and through the length of my days the house of the Lord [and His presence] shall be my dwelling place.

Psalm 23:1-6 AMP

Blessed is the nation whose God is the Lord; and the people whom he hath chosen for his own inheritance.

Psalm 33:12

Behold, the eye of the Lord is upon them that fear him, upon them that hope in his mercy;

To deliver their soul from death, and to keep them alive in famine.

Psalm 33:18,19

The young lions do lack, and suffer hunger: but they that seek the Lord shall not want any good thing.

Psalm 34:10

Apostates may be famishing and starving, but those who turn to the Eternal lack no good.

Psalm 34:10
Moffatt's Trans.

Let them shout for joy, and be glad, that favour my righteous cause: yea, let them say continually, Let the Lord be magnified, which hath pleasure in the prosperity of his servant.

Psalm 35:27

The Lord knoweth the days of the upright: and their inheritance shall be for ever.

They shall not be ashamed in the evil time: and in the days of famine they shall be satisfied.

Psalm 37:18,19

For such as be blessed of him shall inherit the earth.

Psalm 37:22a

I have been young and now I am old. And in all my years I have never seen the Lord forsake a man who loves him; nor have I seen the children of the godly go hungry.

Instead, the godly are able to be generous with their gifts and loans to others, and their children are a blessing.

Psalm 37:25,26 TLB

I have been young and I am old, but never have I seen good men forsaken;

They always have something to give away, something wherewith to bless their families.

Psalm 37:25,26
Moffatt's Trans.

For every beast of the forest is Mine, and the cattle upon a thousand hills or upon the mountains where thousands are.

Psalm 50:10 AMP

If riches increase, set not your heart upon them.

Psalm 62:10b

You let men ride over our heads; we went through fire and water, but you brought us to a place of abundance.

Psalm 66:12 NIV

Then shall the earth yield her increase; and God, even our own God, shall bless us.

God shall bless us; and all the ends of the earth shall fear him.

Psalm 67:6,7

For the Lord God is a sun and shield: the Lord will give grace and glory: no good thing will he withhold from them that walk uprightly.

Psalm 84:11

For Jehovah God is our Light and our Protector. He gives us grace and glory. No good thing will he withhold from those who walk along his paths.

O Lord of the armies of heaven, blessed are those who trust in you.

Psalm 84:11,12 TLB

Give unto the Lord, O ye kindreds of the people, give unto the Lord glory and strength.

Give unto the Lord the glory due unto his name: bring an offering, and come into his courts.

O worship the Lord in the beauty of

holiness: fear before him, all the earth.
Psalm 96:7-9

O Lord, how manifold are thy works! in wisdom hast thou made them all: the earth is full of thy riches.
Psalm 104:24

The Lord made his people very fruitful; he made them too numerous for their foes.
Psalm 105:24 NIV

He brought them forth also with silver and gold: and there was not one feeble person among their tribes.
Psalm 105:37

Then he led out his clansmen, carrying spoil of gold and silver, not a weary man among them.
Psalm 105:37
Moffatt's Trans.

Praise the Lord! Blessed is the man who fears the Lord, who delights greatly in His commandments.

His descendants will be mighty on earth; the generation of the upright will be blessed.

Wealth and riches will be in his house, and his righteousness endures forever.

Unto the upright there arises light in the darkness; he is gracious, and full of compassion, and righteous.

A good man deals graciously and lends; he will guide his affairs with discretion.

Psalm 112:1-5 NKJV

The Lord hath been mindful of us: he will bless us; he will bless the house of Israel; he will bless the house of Aaron.

He will bless them that fear the Lord, both small and great.

The Lord shall increase you more and more, you and your children.

Ye are blessed of the Lord which made heaven and earth.

Psalm 115:12-15

Blessed are the undefiled in the way, who walk in the law of the Lord.

Blessed are they that keep his testimonies, and that seek him with the whole heart.

Psalm 119:1,2

Pray for the peace of Jerusalem: they shall prosper that love thee.

Peace be within thy walls, and prosperity within thy palaces.

Psalm 122:6,7

Blessed is every one who fears the Lord, who walks in His ways.

When you eat the labor of your hands, you shall be happy, and it shall be well with you.

Your wife shall be like a fruitful vine in the very heart of your house, your children like olive plants all around your table.

Behold, thus shall the man be blessed who fears the Lord.

The Lord bless you out of Zion, and may you see the good of Jerusalem all the days of your life.

Yes, may you see your children's children. Peace be upon Israel!

Psalm 128:1-6 NKJV

I will bless her with abundant provisions;
her poor will I satisfy with food.

Psalm 132:15 NIV

Honour the Lord with thy substance, and
with the firstfruits of all thine increase:

So shall thy barns be filled with plenty, and thy presses shall burst out with new
wine.

Proverbs 3:9,10

Happy is the man who finds wisdom, and
the man who gains understanding;

For her proceeds are better than the
profits of silver, and her gain than fine
gold.

She is more precious than rubies, and
all the things you may desire cannot com-
pare with her.

Length of days is in her right hand, in
her left hand riches and honor.

Proverbs 3:13-16 NKJV

Have no fear of sudden disaster or of the
ruin that overtakes the wicked,

For the Lord will be your confidence

The Spirit-Filled Pocket Bible on Finances

and will keep your foot from being snared.

Do not withhold good from those who deserve it, when it is in your power to act.

Do not say to your neighbor, "Come back later; I'll give it tomorrow" — when you now have it with you.

Do not plot harm against your neighbor, who lives trustfully near you.

Do not accuse a man for no reason — when he has done you no harm.

Do not envy a violent man or choose any of his ways,

For the Lord detests a perverse man but takes the upright into his confidence.

The Lord's curse is on the house of the wicked, but he blesses the home of the righteous.

He mocks proud mockers but gives grace to the humble.

The wise inherit honor, but fools he holds up to shame.

Proverbs 3:25-35 NIV

Yet a little sleep, a little slumber, a little folding of the hands to sleep:

58

So shall thy poverty come as one that travelleth, and thy want as an armed man.
Proverbs 6:10,11

Men do not despise a thief, if he steal to satisfy his soul when he is hungry;

But if he be found, he shall restore sevenfold; he shall give all the substance of his house.

Proverbs 6:30,31

Men do not let off a thief, even if he steals to satisfy his hunger; if he is caught, he has to pay for it seven times over.

Proverbs 6:30,31
Moffatt's Trans.

I love those who love me, and those who seek me early and diligently shall find me.

Riches and honor are with me, enduring wealth and righteousness (uprightness in every area and relation, and right standing with God).

My fruit is better than gold, yes, than refined gold, and my increase than choice silver.

I [Wisdom] walk in the way of righteousness (moral and spiritual rectitude in every area and relation), in the midst of the paths of justice,

That I may cause those who love me to inherit [true] riches and that I may fill their treasuries.

Proverbs 8:17-21 AMP

Now therefore listen to me, O you sons; for blessed (happy, fortunate, to be envied) are those who keep my ways.

Hear instruction and be wise, and do not refuse or neglect it.

Blessed (happy, fortunate, to be envied) is the man who listens to me, watching daily at my gates, waiting at the posts of my doors.

For whoever finds me [Wisdom] finds life and draws forth and obtains favor from the Lord.

Proverbs 8:32-35 AMP

The Lord will not suffer the soul of the righteous to famish: but he casteth away the substance of the wicked.

He becometh poor that dealeth with a slack hand: but the hand of the diligent maketh rich.

He that gathereth in summer is a wise son: but he that sleepeth in harvest is a son that causeth shame.

Blessings are upon the head of the just.

Proverbs 10:3-6a

The blessing of the Lord brings wealth, and he adds no trouble to it.

Proverbs 10:22 NIV

It is the blessing of the Lord that makes rich, and He adds no sorrow to it.

Proverbs 10:22 NASB

The desire of the righteous shall be granted.

Proverbs 10:24b

There is one who scatters, yet increases all the more, and there is one who withholds what is justly due, but it results only in want.

The generous man will be prosperous,

and he who waters will himself be watered.

He who withholds grain, the people will curse him, but blessing will be on the head of him who sells it.

He who diligently seeks good seeks favor, but he who searches after evil, it will come to him.

He who trusts in his riches will fall, but the righteous will flourish like the green leaf.

Proverbs 11:24-28 NASB

The hand of the diligent shall bear rule: but the slothful shall be under tribute.

Proverbs 12:24

From the fruit of his lips a man enjoys good things, but the unfaithful have a craving for violence.

He who guards his lips guards his life, but he who speaks rashly will come to ruin.

The sluggard craves and gets nothing, but the desires of the diligent are fully satisfied.

Proverbs 13:2-4 NIV

Wealth gotten by vanity shall be diminished: but he that gathereth by labour shall increase.

Proverbs 13:11

Poverty and shame shall be to him that refuseth instruction: but he that regardeth reproof shall be honoured.

Proverbs 13:18

A good man leaveth an inheritance to his children's children: and the wealth of the sinner is laid up for the just.

Proverbs 13:22

The righteous eateth to the satisfying of his soul: but the belly of the wicked shall want.

Proverbs 13:25

He that hath mercy on the poor, happy is he.

Proverbs 14:21

All hard work brings a profit, but mere

talk leads only to poverty.

Proverbs 14:23 NIV

I the house of the righteous is much treasure: but in the revenues of the wicked is trouble.

Proverbs 15:6

The Lord will destroy the house of the proud: but he will establish the border of the widow.

Proverbs 15:25

He who hates a bribe shall prosper.

Proverbs 15:27b
Moffatt's Trans.

He who is slothful in his work is a brother to him who is a great destroyer.

Proverbs 18:9 NKJV

House and riches are the inheritance of fathers: and a prudent wife is from the Lord.

Slothfulness casteth into a deep sleep; and an idle soul shall suffer hunger.

Proverbs 19:14,15

He who cares for the poor is lending to
the Eternal, and for his kindness he shall
be repaid.

Proverbs 19:17
Moffatt's Trans.

The fear of the Lord tendeth to life: and he
that hath it shall abide satisfied; he shall
not be visited with evil.

A slothful man hideth his hand in his
bosom, and will not so much as bring it to
his mouth again.

Proverbs 19:23,24

The righteous man leads a blameless life;
blessed are his children after him.

Proverbs 20:7 NIV

Love not sleep, lest thou come to poverty;
open thine eyes, and thou shalt be satisfied
with bread.

Proverbs 20:13

The thoughts of the diligent tend only to
plenteousness; but of every one that is
hasty only to want.

Proverbs 21:5

He who is deaf to the cry of the poor, one day his own cry shall not be heard.

> **Proverbs 21:13**
> Moffatt's Trans.

He who loves pleasure will be a poor man; he who loves wine and oil will not be rich.

> **Proverbs 21:17** NKJV

The wise man saves for the future, but the foolish man spends whatever he gets.

> **Proverbs 21:20** TLB

A good name is rather to be chosen than great riches, and loving favor rather than silver and gold.

The rich and poor meet together; the Lord is the Maker of them all...

The reward of humility and the reverent and worshipful fear of the Lord is riches and honor and life.

> **Proverbs 22:1,2,4** AMP

The rich ruleth over the poor, and the borrower is servant to the lender.

> **Proverbs 22:7**

He that hath a bountiful eye shall be blessed; for he giveth of his bread to the poor.

Proverbs 22:9

He that oppresseth the poor to increase his riches, and he that giveth to the rich, shall surely come to want.

Proverbs 22:16

Seest thou a man diligent in his business? he shall stand before kings; he shall not stand before mean men.

Proverbs 22:29

Do you see a man skilled in his work? He will serve before kings; he will not serve before obscure men.

Proverbs 22:29 NIV

Don't weary yourself trying to get rich. Why waste your time? For riches can disappear as though they had the wings of a bird!

Proverbs 23:4,5 TLB

For the drunkard and the glutton shall come to poverty: and drowsiness shall clothe a man with rags.

Proverbs 23:21

Through wisdom a house is built, and by understanding it is established;

By knowledge the rooms are filled with all precious and pleasant riches.

Proverbs 24:3,4 NKJV

I went by the field of the slothful, and by the vineyard of the man void of understanding;

And, lo, it was all grown over with thorns, and nettles had covered the face thereof, and the stone wall thereof was broken down.

Then I saw, and considered it well: I looked upon it, and received instruction.

Yet a little sleep, a little slumber, a little folding of the hands to sleep:

So shall thy poverty come as one that travelleth; and thy want as an armed man.

Proverbs 24:30-34

He that covereth his sins shall not prosper:

but whoso confesseth and forsaketh them
shall have mercy.

Proverbs 28:13

Hard work brings prosperity; playing
around brings poverty.

The man who wants to do right will
get a rich reward. But the man who wants
to get rich quick will quickly fail.

Giving preferred treatment to rich
people is a clear case of selling one's soul
for a piece of bread.

Trying to get rich quick is evil and
leads to poverty.

Proverbs 28:19-22 TLB

He who is of a greedy spirit stirs up strife,
but he who puts his trust in the Lord shall
be enriched and blessed.

Proverbs 28:25 AMP

He who trusts in the Eternal thrives.

Proverbs 28:25b
Moffatt's Trans.

He that giveth unto the poor shall not
lack: but he that hideth his eyes shall have
many a curse.

Proverbs 28:27

The king that faithfully judgeth the poor,
his throne shall be established for ever.
                              Proverbs 29:14

That everyone may eat and drink, and find
satisfaction in all his toil — this is the gift
of God.
                           Ecclesiastes 3:13 NIV

Whoever loves money never has money
enough; whoever loves wealth is never satisfied with his income.
                          Ecclesiastes 5:10 NIV

Every man also to whom God hath given
riches and wealth, and hath given him
power to eat thereof, and to take his portion, and to rejoice in his labour; this is the
gift of God.
                             Ecclesiastes 5:19

A good name is better than precious oint-
ment.
                             Ecclesiastes 7:1a

Because of laziness the building decays,

and through idleness of hands the house leaks.

Ecclesiastes 10:18 NKJV

Cast thy bread upon the waters: for thou shalt find it after many days.

Ecclesiastes 11:1

If ye be willing and obedient, ye shall eat the good of the land:

But if ye refuse and rebel, ye shall be devoured with the sword: for the mouth of the Lord hath spoken it.

Isaiah 1:19,20

He will also send you rain for the seed you sow in the ground, and the food that comes from the land will be rich and plentiful.

Isaiah 30:23a NIV

He who walks righteously and speaks uprightly, he who despises the gain of oppressions, who gestures with his hands, refusing bribes, who stops his ears from hearing of bloodshed, and shuts his eyes from seeing evil:

He will dwell on high; his place of defense will be the fortress of rocks; bread will be given him, his water will be sure.

Isaiah 33:15,16 NKJV

I give waters in the wilderness, and rivers in the desert, to give drink to my people, my chosen.

Isaiah 43:20b

I will go before thee, and make the crooked places straight: I will break in pieces the gates of brass, and cut in sunder the bars of iron:

And I will give thee the treasures of darkness, and hidden riches of secret places, that thou mayest know that I, the Lord, which call thee by thy name, am the God of Israel.

Isaiah 45:2,3

I, even I, have foretold it; yes, I have called him [Cyrus]; I have brought him, and [the Lord] shall make his way prosperous.

Isaiah 48:15 AMP

Thus saith the Lord, thy Redeemer, the

Holy One of Israel; I am the Lord thy God which teacheth thee to profit, which leadeth thee by the way that thou shouldest go.
Isaiah 48:17

Is not this the kind of fasting I have chosen: to loose the chains of injustice and untie the cords of the yoke, to set the oppressed free and break every yoke?

Is it not to share your food with the hungry and to provide the poor wanderer with shelter — when you see the naked, to clothe him, and not to turn away from your own flesh and blood?

Then your light will break forth like the dawn, and your healing will quickly appear; then your righteousness will go before you, and the glory of the Lord will be your rear guard.

Then you will call, and the Lord will answer; you will cry for help, and he will say: Here am I. "If you do away with the yoke of oppression, with the pointing finger and malicious talk,

And if you spend yourselves in behalf of the hungry and satisfy the needs of the oppressed, then your light will rise in the darkness, and your night will become like the noonday.

The Lord will guide you always; he will satisfy your needs in a sun-scorched land and will strengthen your frame. You will be like a well-watered garden, like a spring whose waters never fail.

Your people will rebuild the ancient ruins and will raise up the age-old foundations; you will be called Repairer of Broken Walls, Restorer of Streets with Dwellings.

If you keep your feet from breaking the Sabbath and from doing as you please on my holy day, if you call the Sabbath a delight and the Lord's holy day honorable, and if you honor it by not going your own way and not doing as you please or speaking idle words,

Then you will find your joy in the Lord, and I will cause you to ride on the heights of the land and to feast on the inheritance of your father Jacob." The mouth of the Lord has spoken.

Isaiah 58:6-14 NIV

Arise [from the depression and prostration in which circumstances have kept you — rise to a new life]! Shine (be radiant with the glory of the Lord), for your light has come, and the glory of the Lord has risen upon you!

For behold, darkness shall cover the earth, and dense darkness [all] peoples, but the Lord shall arise upon you [O Jerusalem], and His glory shall be seen on you.

And nations shall come to your light, and kings to the brightness of your rising.

Lift up your eyes round about you and see! They all gather themselves together, they come to you. Your sons shall come from afar, and your daughters shall be carried and nursed in the arms.

Then you shall see and be radiant, and your heart shall thrill and tremble with joy [at the glorious deliverance] and be enlarged; because the abundant wealth of the [Dead] Sea shall be turned to you, unto you shall the nations come with their treasures.

A multitude of camels [from the eastern trading tribes] shall cover you [Jerusalem], the young camels of Midian and Ephah; all the men from Sheba [who once came to trade] shall come, bringing gold and frankincense and proclaiming the praises of the Lord.

All the flocks of Kedar shall be gathered to you [as the eastern pastoral tribes join the trading tribes], the rams of Nebaioth shall minister to you; they shall come up with acceptance on My altar, and My glorious house I will glorify.

Isaiah 60:1-7 AMP

They shall not build, and another inhabit; they shall not plant, and another eat: for as the days of a tree are the days of my people, and mine elect shall long enjoy the work of their hands.

They shall not labour in vain, nor bring forth for trouble; for they are the seed of the blessed of the Lord, and their offspring with them.

And it shall come to pass, that before they call, I will answer; and while they are yet speaking, I will hear.

Isaiah 65:22-24

Blessed is the man that trusteth in the

Lord, and whose hope the Lord is.

For he shall be as a tree planted by the waters, and that spreadeth out her roots by the river, and shall not see when heat cometh, but her leaf shall be green; and shall not be careful in the year of drought, neither shall cease from yielding fruit.

Jeremiah 17:7,8

"He defended the cause of the poor and needy, and so all went well. Is that not what it means to know me?" declares the Lord.

Jeremiah 22:16 NIV

"For I know the plans I have for you," declares the Lord, "plans to prosper you and not to harm you, plans to give you hope and a future."

Jeremiah 29:11 NIV

Behold, therefore, I beat My fists at the dishonest profit which you have made.

Ezekiel 22:13 NKJV

Then you shall dwell in the land that I

gave to your fathers; you shall be My people, and I will be your God.

I will deliver you from all your uncleannesses. I will call for the grain and multiply it, and bring no famine upon you.

And I will multiply the fruit of your trees and the increase of your fields, so that you need never again bear the reproach of famine among the nations.

Ezekiel 36:28-30 NKJV

My people are destroyed for lack of knowledge.

Hosea 4:6a

Fear not, O land; be glad and rejoice: for the Lord will do great things.

Be not afraid, ye beasts of the field: for the pastures of the wilderness do spring, for the tree beareth her fruit, the fig tree and the vine do yield their strength.

Be glad then, ye children of Zion, and rejoice in the Lord your God: for he hath given you the former rain moderately, and he will cause to come down for you the rain, the former rain, and the latter rain in the first month.

And the floors shall be full of wheat, and the fats shall overflow with wine and oil.

And I will restore to you the years that the locust hath eaten, the cankerworm, and the caterpiller, and the palmerworm, my great army which I sent among you.

And ye shall eat in plenty, and be satisfied, and praise the name of the Lord your God, that hath dealt wondrously with you: and my people shall never be ashamed.

And ye shall know that I am in the midst of Israel, and that I am the Lord your God, and none else: and my people shall never be ashamed.

Joel 2:21-27

For the seed shall be prosperous; the vine shall give her fruit, and the ground shall give her increase, and the heavens shall give their dew; and I will cause the remnant of this people to possess all these things.

Zechariah 8:12

For I am the Lord, I change not; therefore ye sons of Jacob are not consumed.

Even from the days of your fathers ye are gone away from mine ordinances, and have not kept them. Return unto me, and I will return unto you, saith the Lord of hosts. But ye said, Wherein shall we return?

Will a man rob God? Yet ye have robbed me. But ye say, Wherein have we robbed thee? In tithes and offerings.

Ye are cursed with a curse: for ye have robbed me, even this whole nation.

Bring ye all the tithes into the storehouse, that there may be meat in mine house, and prove me now herewith, saith the Lord of hosts, if I will not open you the windows of heaven, and pour you out a blessing, that there shall not be room enough to receive it.

And I will rebuke the devourer for your sakes, and he shall not destroy the fruits of your ground; neither shall your vine cast her fruit before the time in the field, saith the Lord of hosts.

And all nations shall call you blessed:

for ye shall be a delightsome land, saith
the Lord of hosts.

Malachi 3:6-12

Thy kingdom come. Thy will be done in
earth, as it is in heaven.

Give us this day our daily bread.

Matthew 6:10,11

Lay not up for yourselves treasures upon
earth, where moth and rust doth corrupt,
and where thieves break through and steal:

But lay up for yourselves treasures in
heaven, where neither moth nor rust doth
corrupt, and where thieves do not break
through nor steal:

For where your treasure is, there will
your heart be also.

Matthew 6:19-21

Therefore I say to you, do not worry about
your life, what you will eat or what you
will drink; nor about your body, what you
will put on. Is not life more than food and
the body more than clothing?

Look at the birds of the air, for they

neither sow nor reap nor gather into barns; yet your heavenly Father feeds them. Are you not of more value than they?

Which of you by worrying can add one cubit to his stature?

So why do you worry about clothing? Consider the lilies of the field, how they grow: they neither toil nor spin;

And yet I say to you that even Solomon in all his glory was not arrayed like one of these.

Now if God so clothes the grass of the field, which today is, and tomorrow is thrown into the oven, will He not much more clothe you, O you of little faith?

Therefore do not worry, saying, "What shall we eat?" or "What shall we drink?" or "What shall we wear?"

For after all these things the Gentiles seek. For your heavenly Father knows that you need all these things.

But seek first the kingdom of God and His righteousness, and all these things shall be added to you.

Therefore do not worry about tomorrow, for tomorrow will worry about its own things. Sufficient for the day is its own trouble.

Matthew 6:25-34 NKJV

But he that received seed into the good ground is he that heareth the word, and understandeth it; which also beareth fruit, and bringeth forth, some an hundredfold, some sixty, and some thirty.

Matthew 13:23

After Jesus and his disciples arrived in Capernaum, the collectors of the two-drachma tax came to Peter and asked, "Doesn't your teacher pay the temple tax?"

"Yes, he does," he replied.

When Peter came into the house, Jesus was the first to speak. "What do you think, Simon?" he asked. "From whom do the kings of the earth collect duty and taxes — from their own sons or from others?"

"From others," Peter answered.

"Then the sons are exempt," Jesus said to him. "But so that we may not offend them, go to the lake and throw out your line. Take the first fish you catch; open its mouth and you will find a four-drachma coin. Take it and give it to them for my tax and yours."

Matthew 17:24-27 NIV

Therefore, the Kingdom of Heaven was likened to a king who wished to make a reckoning with his servants.

And, when he began to reckon, there was brought to him one debtor of ten thousand talents;

But, as he had nothing to pay, his lord commanded that he be sold, and his wife, and his children, and all that he had, and payment to be made.

The servant, falling down, therefore, was bowing to him, saying, "Lord, have patience with me, and I will pay you all."

And, moved with compassion, the lord of that servant released him, and forgave him the debt.

But, going forth, that servant found one of his fellow-servants, who was owing him a hundred denaries; and, having laid hold of him, he was choking him, saying, "Pay, if you are owing anything!"

His fellow-servant, falling down,

therefore, was entreating him, saying, "Have patience with me, and I will pay you!"

And he would not; but, going away, he cast him into prison, till he should pay what was due.

Therefore, his fellow-servants, seeing what was done, were exceedingly grieved; and, going, they made known to their lord all that was done.

Then, calling him to him, his lord says to him, "Evil servant! I forgave you all that debt, because you besought me.

"Should you not also have had mercy on your fellow-servant, as I had mercy on you?"

And, being angry, his lord delivered him to the tormentors, until he should pay all the debt.

So also will My Heavenly Father do to you, if ye forgive not, each one his brother, from your hearts.

Matthew 18:23-35
The Worrell New Testament

And, behold, one, having come near, said to Him, "Teacher, what good thing shall I do, that I may have eternal life?"

And He said to him, "Why do you question Me concerning the good? One is the Good. But, if you wish to enter into life, keep the commandments."

He says to Him, "Which?" And Jesus said, "You shall not kill; you shall not commit adultery; you shall not steal; you shall not bear false witness;

"Honor your father and your mother; and, you shall love your neighbor as yourself."

The young man says to Him, "I observed all these things; what yet do I lack?"

Jesus said to him, "If you wish to be perfect, go, sell what you have, and give to the poor, and you shall have treasure in Heaven; and come, follow Me." But the young man, having heard this saying, went away grieved; for he was one who had large possessions.

And Jesus said to His disciples, "Verily I say to you, that with difficulty shall a rich man enter into the Kingdom of Heaven. And again I say to you, It is easier for a camel to go through the eye of a needle than for a rich man to enter into the Kingdom of God."

And the disciples, having heard it, were amazed exceedingly, saying, "Who, then, can be saved?"

But Jesus, looking on them, said to them, "With men this is impossible, but with God all things are possible."

Then Peter, answering, said to Him, "Behold, we left all, and followed Thee; what, then, shall we have?"

And Jesus said to them, "Verily I say to you, that ye who followed Me, in the regeneration, when the Son of Man shall sit upon the throne of His glory, ye also shall sit upon twelve thrones, judging the twelve tribes of Israel. And every one who left houses, or brothers, or sisters, or father, or mother, or children, or lands, for My name's sake, shall receive manifold more and shall inherit eternal life."

Matthew 19:16-29
The Worrell New Testament

For the kingdom of heaven is as a man travelling into a far country, who called his own servants, and delivered unto them his goods.

And unto one he gave five talents, to another two, and to another one; to every man according to his several ability; and straightway took his journey.

Then he that had received the five talents went and traded with the same, and made them other five talents.

And likewise he that had received two, he also gained other two.

But he that had received one went and digged in the earth, and hid his lord's money.

After a long time the lord of those servants cometh, and reckoneth with them.

And so he that had received five talents came and brought other five talents, saying, Lord, thou deliveredst unto me five talents: behold, I have gained beside them five talents more.

His lord said unto him, Well done, thou good and faithful servant: thou hast been faithful over a few things, I will make thee ruler over many things: enter thou into the joy of thy lord.

He also that had received two talents came and said, Lord, thou deliveredst unto me two talents: behold, I have gained two other talents beside them.

His lord said unto him, Well done, good and faithful servant; thou hast been faithful over a few things, I will make thee ruler over many things: enter thou into the joy of thy lord.

Then he which had received the one talent came and said, Lord, I knew thee that thou art an hard man, reaping where thou hast not sown, and gathering where thou hast not strawed:

And I was afraid, and went and hid thy talent in the earth: lo, there thou hast that is thine.

His lord answered and said unto him, Thou wicked and slothful servant, thou knewest that I reap where I sowed not, and gather where I have not strawed:

Thou oughtest therefore to have put my money to the exchangers, and then at my coming I should have received mine own with usury.

Take therefore the talent from him, and give it unto him which hath ten talents.

For unto every one that hath shall be given, and he shall have abundance: but from him that hath not shall be taken away even that which he hath.

Matthew 25:14-29

And the cares of this world, and the deceitfulness of riches, and the lusts of other things entering in, choke the word, and it becometh unfruitful.

Mark 4:19

"If anyone has ears to hear, let him hear."

Then He said to them, "Take heed what you hear. With the same measure you use, it will be measured to you; and to you who hear, more will be given.

"For whoever has, to him more will be given; but whoever does not have, even what he has will be taken away from him."

And He said, "The kingdom of God is as if a man should scatter seed on the ground,

"And should sleep by night and rise by day, and the seed should sprout and grow, he himself does not know how.

"For the earth yields crops by itself: first the blade, then the head, after that the full grain in the head.

"But when the grain ripens, immediately he puts in the sickle, because the harvest has come."

Mark 4:23-29 NKJV

When it grew late, his disciples came up to him, and said: "This is a lonely spot, and it is already late. Send the people away, so that they may go to the farms and villages around and buy themselves something to eat."

But Jesus said: "It is for you to give them something to eat."

"Are we to go and buy two hundred pounds worth of bread," they asked, "to give them to eat?"

"How many loaves have you?" he asked; "go, and see." When they had found out, they told him: "Five, and two fishes." Jesus directed them to make all the people take their seats on the green grass, in parties; and they sat down in groups — in hundreds, and in fifties. Taking the five loaves and the two fishes, Jesus looked up

to Heaven, and said the blessing; he broke
the loaves into pieces, and gave them to his
disciples for them to serve out to the people, and he divided the two fishes also
among them all. Every one had sufficient
to eat; and they picked up enough broken
pieces to fill twelve baskets, as well as some
of the fish. The men who ate the bread
were five thousand in number.

Mark 6:35-44
The Twentieth Century
New Testament

And Jesus answered and said, Verily I say
unto you, There is no man that hath left
house, or brethren, or sisters, or father, or
mother, or wife, or children, or lands, for
my sake, and the gospel's,

But he shall receive an hundredfold
now in this time, houses, and brethren,
and sisters, and mothers, and children, and
lands, with persecutions; and in the world
to come eternal life.

Mark 10:29,30

"Have faith in God," Jesus answered. "I tell
you the truth, if anyone says to this moun-

tain, 'Go, throw yourself into the sea,' and does not doubt in his heart but believes that what he says will happen, it will be done for him. Therefore I tell you, whatever you ask for in prayer, believe that you have received it, and it will be yours."

Mark 11:22-24 NIV

Then Jesus sat down opposite the chests for the Temple offerings, and watched how the people put money into them. Many rich people were putting in large sums; but one poor widow came and put in two coins, together worth less than a halfpenny.

On this, calling his disciples to him, Jesus said:

"I tell you that this poor widow has put in more than all the others who were putting money into the chests; for every one else put in something from what he had to spare, while she, in her need, put in all she had — everything that she had to live on."

Mark 12:41-44
The Twentieth Century
New Testament

93

Now it came to pass, as the multitude was pressing upon Him, and hearing the word of God, that He was standing by the lake Gennesaret; and He saw two boats standing by the lake; but the fishermen, having gone out of them, were washing their nets. And, entering into one of the boats, which was Simon's, He asked him to put out a little from the land; and, having taken a seat, He was teaching the multitudes out of the boat.

And, when He ceased speaking, He said to Simon, "Put out into the deep, and let down your nets for a draught."

And Simon, answering, said, "Master, having toiled through the whole night, we took nothing; but at Thy word I will let down the nets." And, doing this, they enclosed a great multitude of fishes; and their nets were breaking. And they beckoned to their partners in the other boat, to come and help them. And they came, and filled both the boats, so that they were sinking.

And Simon Peter, seeing it, fell down at the knees of Jesus, saying, "Depart from

me; because I am a sinful man, O Lord;"
for astonishment seized him, and all those
with him, on account of the draught of
the fishes which they took; and likewise
also James and John, sons of Zebedee, who
were partners with Simon.

And Jesus said to Simon, "Fear not;
henceforth you will catch men." And, having brought their boats to the land, leaving
all, they followed Him.

Luke 5:1-11
The Worrell New Testament

Give, and it will be given to you: good
measure, pressed down, shaken together,
and running over will be put into your
bosom. For with the same measure that
you use, it will be measured back to you.

Luke 6:38 NKJV

Be constantly giving, and it shall be given
you, a generous measure that has been
pressed down hard and which has been
shaken thoroughly and which is running
over shall they give into the pouch of your
outer garment, for with the measure by

which you are accustomed to measure, it shall be measured to you again.

Luke 6:38

The Wuest New Testament

Give and men will give to you — yes, good measure, pressed down, shaken together and running over will they pour into your lap. For whatever measure you use with other people, they will use in their dealings with you.

Luke 6:38

J. B. Phillips Trans.

Then Jesus answered and said: "A certain man went down from Jerusalem to Jericho, and fell among thieves, who stripped him, and departed, leaving him half dead.

"Now by chance a certain priest came down that road. And when he saw him, he passed by on the other side.

"Likewise a Levite, when he arrived at the place, came and looked, and passed by on the other side.

"But a certain Samaritan, as he jour-neyed, came where he was. And when he saw him, he had compassion.

"So he went to him and bandaged his wounds, pouring on oil and wine; and he set him on his own animal, brought him to an inn, and took care of him.

"On the next day, when he departed, he took out two denarii, gave them to the innkeeper, and said to him, 'Take care of him; and whatever more you spend, when I come again, I will repay you.'

"So which of these three do you think was neighbor to him who fell among the thieves?"

And he said, "He who showed mercy on him." Then Jesus said to him, "Go and do likewise."

Luke 10:30-37 NKJV

But woe to you Pharisees! you tithe mint and rue and every vegetable, but justice and the love of God you disregard; these latter you ought to have practised — without omitting the former.

Luke 11:42
Moffatt's Trans.

Then he said to them, "Watch out! Be on

your guard against all kinds of greed; a man's life does not consist in the abundance of his possessions."

And he told them this parable: "The ground of a certain rich man produced a good crop. He thought to himself, 'What shall I do? I have no place to store my crops.'

"Then he said, 'This is what I'll do. I will tear down my barns and build bigger ones, and there I will store all my grain and my goods. And I'll say to myself, "You have plenty of good things laid up for many years. Take life easy; eat, drink and be merry."'

"But God said to him, 'You fool! This very night your life will be demanded from you. Then who will get what you have prepared for yourself?'

"This is how it will be with anyone who stores up things for himself but is not rich toward God."

Then Jesus said to his disciples: "Therefore I tell you, do not worry about your life, what you will eat; or about your body, what you will wear. Life is more than food, and the body more than clothes.

Consider the ravens: They do not sow or reap, but have no storeroom or barn; yet God feeds them. And how much more valuable you are than birds! Who of you by worrying can add a single hour to his life? Since you cannot do this very little thing, why do you worry about the rest?

"Consider how the lilies grow. They do not labor or spin. Yet I tell you, not even Solomon in all his splendor was dressed like one of these. If that is how God clothes the grass of the field, which is here today, and tomorrow is thrown into the fire, how much more will he clothe you, O you of little faith! And do not set your heart on what you will eat or drink; do not worry about it. For the pagan world runs after all such things, and your Father knows that you need them. But seek his kingdom, and these things will be given to you as well.

"Do not be afraid, little flock, for your Father has been pleased to give you the kingdom. Sell your possessions and give to the poor. Provide purses for yourselves that will not wear out, a treasure in heaven that will not be exhausted, where no thief comes near and no moth destroys. For where your treasure is, there your heart will be also.

Luke 12:15-34 NIV

And when they wanted wine, the mother of Jesus saith unto him, They have no wine.

Jesus saith unto her, Woman, what have I to do with thee? mine hour is not yet come.

His mother saith unto the servants, Whatsoever he saith unto you, do it.

And there were set there six waterpots of stone, after the manner of the purifying of the Jews, containing two or three firkins apiece.

Jesus saith unto them, Fill the waterpots with water. And they filled them up to the brim.

And he saith unto them, Draw out now, and bear unto the governor of the feast. And they bare it.

When the ruler of the feast had tasted the water that was made wine, and knew not whence it was: (but the servants which drew the water knew;) the governor of the feast called the bridegroom,

And saith unto him, Every man at the beginning doth set forth good wine; and when men have well drunk, then that which is worse: but thou hast kept the good wine until now.

John 2:3-10

On looking up and seeing a large crowd approach, he said to Philip, "Where are we to buy bread for all these people to eat?" (He said this to test Philip, for he knew what he was going to do himself.) Philip answered, "Seven pounds' worth of bread would not be enough for them, for everybody to get even a morsel."

One of his disciples, Andrew the brother of Simon Peter, said to him, "There is a servant here, with five barley-cakes and a couple of fish; but what is that among so many?"

Jesus said, "Get the people to lie down." Now there was plenty of grass at the spot, so the men lay down, numbering about five thousand.

Then Jesus took the loaves, gave

thanks to God, and distributed them to those who were reclining; so too with the fish, as much as they wanted.

And when they were satisfied, he said to the disciples, "Gather up the pieces left over, so that nothing may be wasted."

They gathered them up, and filled twelve baskets with pieces of the five loaves left over from the meal.

John 6:5-13
Moffatt's Trans.

All of us must quickly carry out the tasks assigned us by the one who sent me, for there is little time left before the night falls and all work comes to an end.

John 9:4 TLB

The thief does not come except to steal, and to kill, and to destroy. I have come that they may have life, and that they may have it more abundantly.

John 10:10 NKJV

The thief comes only to steal, to kill, and to destroy; I have come that they may have

Life, and may have it in greater fulness.

John 10:10

The Twentieth Century
New Testament

Afterward Jesus appeared again to his disciples, by the Sea of Tiberias. It happened this way: Simon Peter, Thomas (called Didymus), Nathanael from Cana in Galilee, the sons of Zebedee, and two other disciples were together. "I'm going out to fish," Simon Peter told them, and they said, "We'll go with you." So they went out and got into the boat, but that night they caught nothing.

Early in the morning, Jesus stood on the shore, but the disciples did not realize that it was Jesus.

He called out to them, "Friends, haven't you any fish?"

"No," they answered.

He said, "Throw your net on the right side of the boat and you will find some." When they did, they were unable to haul the net in because of the large number of fish.

Then the disciple whom Jesus loved said to Peter, "It is the Lord!" As soon as Simon Peter heard him say, "It is the Lord," he wrapped his outer garment around him (for he had taken it off) and jumped into the water. The other disciples followed in the boat, towing the net full of fish, for they were not far from shore, about a hundred yards. When they landed, they saw a fire of burning coals there with fish on it, and some bread.

Jesus said to them, "Bring some of the fish you have just caught."

Simon Peter climbed aboard and dragged the net ashore. It was full of large fish, 153, but even with so many the net was not torn. Jesus said to them, "Come and have breakfast." None of the disciples dared ask him, "Who are you?" They knew it was the Lord. Jesus came, took the bread and gave it to them, and did the same with the fish. This was now the third time Jesus appeared to his disciples after he was raised from the dead.

John 21:1-14 NIV

The Apostles continued with great power

to bear their testimony to the resurrection
of the Lord Jesus, and God's blessing rest-
ed upon them all abundantly. Nor was
there any one in need among them, for all
who were owners of land or houses sold
them, and brought the proceeds of the
sales and laid them at the Apostles' feet;
and then every one received a share in
proportion to his wants.

A Levite of Cyprian birth, named
Joseph, (who had received from the
Apostles the additional name of 'Barnabas'
— which means 'The Consoler,') sold a
farm that belonged to him, and brought
the money and laid it at the Apostles' feet.

Acts 4:33-37
The Twentieth Century
New Testament

At Caesarea there was a man named
Cornelius, a centurion in what was known
as the Italian Regiment. He and all his
family were devout and God-fearing; he
gave generously to those in need and
prayed to God regularly. One day at about
three in the afternoon he had a vision. He
distinctly saw an angel of God, who came

to him and said, "Cornelius!"

Cornelius stared at him in fear. "What is it, Lord?" he asked.

The angel answered, "Your prayers and gifts to the poor have come up as a memorial offering before God."

Acts 10:1-4 NIV

And now, brethren, I commend you to God, and to the word of his grace, which is able to build you up, and to give you an inheritance among all them which are sanctified.

I have coveted no man's silver, or gold, or apparel.

Yea, ye yourselves know, that these hands have ministered unto my necessities, and to them that were with me.

I have shewed you all things, how that so labouring ye ought to support the weak, and to remember the words of the Lord Jesus, how he said, It is more blessed to give than to receive.

Acts 20:32-35

And now, as to the present things, I com-

mend you to the Lord and to the word of
His grace which has power to build you
up, and to give you the inheritance among
all those who have been set apart for God.

Not even one person's silver or gold
or apparel did I covet. You yourselves
know from experience that these hands
ministered to my necessities and to the
necessities of those with me. In all things I
gave you an example, that in this manner,
working to the point of exhaustion, it is a
necessity in the nature of the case to lend a
helping hand yourselves to those who are
weak, helping them to help themselves in
their difficulties, and to be remembering
the words of the Lord Jesus, that He
Himself said, There is more spiritual prosperity in constantly giving than in constantly receiving.

Acts 20:32-35
The Wuest New Testament

Render therefore to all their dues: tribute
to whom tribute is due; custom to whom
custom; fear to whom fear; honour to
whom honour.

Owe no man any thing, but to love

one another: for he that loveth another hath fulfilled the law.

Romans 13:7,8

"What eye never saw, nor ear ever heard, what never entered the mind of man — even all that God has prepared for those who love him."

Yet to us God revealed it through his Spirit; for the Spirit fathoms all things, even the inmost depths of God's being.

For what man is there who knows what a man is, except the man's own spirit within him? So, also, no one comprehends what God is, except the Spirit of God.

And as for us, it is not the spirit of the World that we have received, but the Spirit that comes from God, that we may realize the blessings given to us by him.

And we speak of these gifts, not in language taught by human philosophy, but in language taught by the Spirit, explaining spiritual things in spiritual words.

The merely intellectual man rejects the teaching of the Spirit of God; for to him it is mere folly; he cannot grasp it, because it is to be understood only by spiritual insight.

But the man with spiritual insight is able to understand everything, although he himself is understood by no one.

For "who has so comprehended the mind of the Lord as to be able to instruct him?" We, however, have the very mind of Christ.

> *1 Corinthians 2:9-16*
> *The Twentieth Century*
> *New Testament*

Upon the first day of the week let every one of you lay by him in store, as God hath prospered him, that there be no gatherings when I come.

And when I come, whomsoever ye shall approve by your letters, them will I send to bring your liberality unto Jerusalem.

> *1 Corinthians 16:2,3*

But this I say, He which soweth sparingly shall reap also sparingly; and he which soweth bountifully shall reap also bountifully.

Every man according as he purposeth

in his heart, so let him give; not grudgingly, or of necessity: for God loveth a cheerful giver.

And God is able to make all grace abound toward you; that ye, always having all sufficiency in all things, may abound to every good work:

(As it is written, He hath dispersed abroad; he hath given to the poor: his righteousness remaineth for ever.

Now he that ministereth seed to the sower both minister bread for your food, and multiply your seed sown, and increase the fruits of your righteousness;)

Being enriched in every thing to all bountifulness, which causeth through us thanksgiving to God.

For the administration of this service not only supplieth the want of the saints, but is abundant also by many thanksgivings unto God.

2 Corinthians 9:6-12

So then they which be of faith are blessed with faithful Abraham.

For as many as are of the works of the

law are under the curse: for it is written,
Cursed is every one that continueth not in
all things which are written in the book of
the law to do them.

But that no man is justified by the law
in the sight of God, it is evident: for, The
just shall live by faith.

And the law is not of faith: but, The
man that doeth them shall live in them.

Christ hath redeemed us from the
curse of the law, being made a curse for us:
for it is written, Cursed is every one that
hangeth on a tree:

That the blessing of Abraham might
come on the Gentiles through Jesus
Christ; that we might receive the promise
of the Spirit through faith.

And if ye be Christ's then are ye
Abraham's seed, and heirs according to the
promise.

Galatians 3:9-14,29

Be not deceived; God is not mocked: for
whatsoever a man soweth, that shall he
also reap.

For he that soweth to his flesh shall of
the flesh reap corruption; but he that

soweth to the Spirit shall of the Spirit reap life everlasting.

And let us not be weary in well doing: for in due season we shall reap, if we faint not.

As we have therefore opportunity, let us do good unto all men, especially unto them who are of the household of faith.

Galatians 6:7-10

Make no mistake — God is not to be mocked — a man will reap just what he sows; he who sows for his flesh will reap destruction for the flesh, and he who sows from the Spirit will reap life eternal from the Spirit.

Never let us grow tired of doing what is right, for if we do not faint we shall reap our harvest at the opportune season. So then, as we have opportunity, let us do good to all men and in particular to the household of faith.

Galatians 6:7-10
Moffatt's Trans.

Let him that stole steal no more: but rather let him labour, working with his hands the thing which is good, that he may have to give to him that needeth.

Ephesians 4:28

I rejoice greatly in the Lord that at last you have renewed your concern for me. Indeed, you have been concerned, but you had no opportunity to show it.

I am not saying this because I am in need, for I have learned to be content whatever the circumstances.

I know what it is to be in need, and I know what it is to have plenty. I have learned the secret of being content in any and every situation, whether well fed or hungry, whether living in plenty or in want.

I can do everything through him who gives me strength.

Yet it was good of you to share in my troubles.

Moreover, as you Philippians know, in the early days of your acquaintance with the gospel, when I set out from Macedonia, not one church shared with me in the matter of giving and receiving, except you only;

For even when I was in Thessalonica, you sent me aid again and again when I was in need.

Not that I am looking for a gift, but I am looking for what may be credited to your account.

I have received full payment and even more; I am amply supplied, now that I have received from Epaphroditus the gifts you sent. They are a fragrant offering, an acceptable sacrifice, pleasing to God.

And my God will meet all your needs according to his glorious riches in Christ Jesus.

Philippians 4:10-19 NIV

Make it your ambition to lead a quiet life and attend to your own business and work with your hands, just as we commanded you;

So that you may behave properly toward outsiders and not be in any need.

1 Thessalonians 4:11,12 NASB

Now we command you, brethren, in the name of our Lord Jesus Christ, that ye withdraw yourselves from every brother that walketh disorderly, and not after the tradition which he received of us.

For yourselves know how ye ought to follow us: for we behaved not ourselves disorderly among you;

Neither did we eat any man's bread for nought; but wrought with labour and travail night and day, that we might not be chargeable to any of you:

Not because we have not power, but to make ourselves an ensample unto you to follow us.

For even when we were with you, this we commanded you, that if any would not work, neither should he eat.

For we hear that there are some which walk among you disorderly, working not at all, but are busybodies.

Now them that are such we command and exhort by our Lord Jesus Christ, that with quietness they work, and eat their own bread.

2 Thessalonians 3:6-12

But if any provide not for his own, and

specially for those of his own house, he hath denied the faith, and is worse than an infidel.

1 Timothy 5:8

Any one who fails to provide for his own relations, and especially for those under his own roof, has disowned the Faith, and is worse than an unbeliever.

1 Timothy 5:8
The Twentieth Century
New Testament

But godliness with contentment is great gain.

For we brought nothing into this world, and it is certain we can carry nothing out.

And having food and raiment let us be therewith content.

But they that will be rich fall into temptation and a snare, and into many foolish and hurtful lusts, which drown men in destruction and perdition.

For the love of money is the root of all evil: which while some coveted after, they have erred from the faith, and pierced themselves through with many sorrows.

1 Timothy 6:6-10

Command those who are rich in this present world not to be arrogant nor to put their hope in wealth, which is so uncertain, but to put their hope in God, who richly provides us with everything for our enjoyment. Command them to do good, to be rich in good deeds, and to be generous and willing to share. In this way they will lay up treasure for themselves as a firm foundation for the coming age, so that they may take hold of the life that is truly life.

1 Timothy 6:17-19 NIV

That ye be not slothful, but followers of them who through faith and patience inherit the promises.

For when God made promise to Abraham, because he could swear by no greater, he sware by himself,

Saying, Surely blessing I will bless thee, and multiplying I will multiply thee.

And so, after he had patiently endured, he obtained the promise.

Hebrews 6:12-15

For this Melchizedek, king of Salem, priest of the Most High God, who met Abraham returning from the slaughter of the kings and blessed him,

To whom also Abraham gave a tenth part of all, first being translated "king of righteousness," and then also king of Salem, meaning "king of peace,"

Without father, without mother, without genealogy, having neither beginning of days nor end of life, but made like the Son of God, remains a priest continually.

Now consider how great this man was, to whom even the patriarch Abraham gave a tenth of the spoils.

And indeed those who are of the sons of Levi, who receive the priesthood, have a commandment to receive tithes from the people according to the law, that is, from their brethren, though they have come from the loins of Abraham;

But he whose genealogy is not derived from them received tithes from Abraham and blessed him who had the promises.

Now beyond all contradiction the lesser is blessed by the better.

Here mortal men receive tithes, but

there he receives them, of whom it is witnessed that he lives...

For it is evident that our Lord arose from Judah, of which tribe Moses spoke nothing concerning priesthood.

And it is yet far more evident if, in the likeness of Melchizedek, there arises another priest

Who has come, not according to the law of a fleshly commandment, but according to the power of an endless life...

By so much more Jesus has become a surety of a better covenant.

Hebrews 7:1-8,14-16,22 NKJV

Beloved, I wish above all things that thou mayest prosper and be in health, even as thy soul prospereth.

3 John 2

Beloved, I pray that you may prosper in every way and [that your body] may keep well, even as [I know] your soul keeps well and prospers.

3 John 2 AMP

After this I looked, and, behold, a door

was opened in heaven: and the first voice which I heard was as it were of a trumpet talking with me; which said, Come up hither, and I will shew thee things which must be hereafter.

And immediately I was in the spirit: and, behold, a throne was set in heaven, and one sat on the throne.

And he that sat was to look upon like a jasper and a sardine stone: and there was a rainbow round about the throne, in sight like unto an emerald.

And round about the throne were four and twenty seats: and upon the seats I saw four and twenty elders, sitting, clothed in white raiment; and they had on their heads crowns of gold.

Revelation 4:1-4

He that overcometh shall inherit all things; and I will be his God, and he shall be my son.

Revelation 21:7

And the building of the wall of it was of jasper: and the city was pure gold, like unto clear glass.

And the foundations of the wall of the city were garnished with all manner of precious stones. The first foundation was jasper; the second, sapphire; the third, a chalcedony; the fourth, an emerald;

The fifth, sardonyx; the sixth, sardius; the seventh, chrysolyte; the eighth, beryl; the ninth, a topaz; the tenth, a chrysoprasus; the eleventh, a jacinth; the twelfth, an amethyst.

And the twelve gates were twelve pearls; every several gate was of one pearl: and the street of the city was pure gold, as it were transparent glass.

Revelation 21:18-21

And, behold, I come quickly; and my reward is with me, to give every man according as his work shall be.

I am Alpha and Omega, the beginning and the end, the first and the last.

Blessed are they that do his commandments, that they may have right to the tree of life, and may enter in through the gates into the city.

Revelation 22:12-14

References

*Other Harrison House
Spirit-Filled Pocket Bibles*

*The Spirit-Filled Pocket Bible on Faith
The Spirit-Filled Pocket Bible on Healing
The Spirit-Filled Pocket Bible on Protection*

*Available from your local
bookstore*

HARRISON HOUSE
Tulsa, Oklahoma 74153

In Canada books are available from:

Word Alive
P. O. Box 670
Niverville, Manitoba
CANADA R0A 1E0

The Harrison House Vision

Proclaiming the truth and the power
Of the Gospel of Jesus Christ
With excellence;

Challenging Christians to
Live victoriously,
Grow spiritually,
Know God intimately.